Stepping Stones

Faith At The Breaking Point

JOANNA BIRCHETT

Stepping Stones: Faith At The Breaking Point

Copyright © July 2014 by Joanna Birchett

Published in the United States of America by

Gospel 4 U Publishing

Edited by Pastor Larry Birchett, Jr.

All rights reserved. No part of this book may be reproduced or transmitted in anyway by means, electronic, mechanical, Photocopy, recording or otherwise, without prior permission of the author except as provided by USA copyright law.
Scriptures are taken from the
King James Version unless otherwise marked.

ISBN: 978-0692023525

Library of Congress Control Number: 2014906819

**Printed in United States of America
July 2014**

JOANNA BIRCHETT

CONTENT

Foreword..*v*

Dedication..9

Acknowledgement......................................11

Introduction...13

1. The Stepping Stones................................15
2. Stepping into Purpose.............................19
3. Silence Is Golden....................................23
4. Faith Crawlers..27
5. Faith Talkers..31
6. Faith Walkers 35
7. Faith To Trust 39
8. Stepping Forward..................................43
9. Get Better Not Bitter............................47
10. Stepping Over Temptation..................51
11. Surrender You.....................................55
12. Character Is Key..................................59
13. Victory is Mine....................................63

21 Days Devotional and Declaration.

FOREWORD

If you were to survey 100 people many would tell you that life has not been easy. Plagued with consequences of poor choices they have made or affected by poor choices others have made, some may wish life had a Do-over button. Think about that for a minute. Wouldn't that be great? Born to the wrong parents? Had a bad childhood? Got involved with the wrong person? Made some bad decisions? No problem just hit the Do-over button. Unfortunately, life has no Do-over buttons but fortunately no matter how bad our lives have been or are, God is able to turn all of those negative bad experiences around for our good and His glory. In fact everything we have been through in the past has made us who we are right now. Even if you have been through some horrible times in life the fact that you are still here is reason enough to praise the Lord because it shows you are a survivor and the Lord has purpose for your life. If we had not gone through bad times how could we ever really appreciate how good life with God is? Only He could exchange beauty for ashes and turn stumbling blocks into stepping stones.

Many times, we fail to see how everything we have gone through or may be currently going through can be used as a stepping-stone. Naturally, speaking a stepping-stone is something that you step on and it takes you a little higher than you were before. Some body say elevation! The more stepping-stones you climb the higher you will find yourself, if you keep stepping. Spiritually we can see this same principle. The more you grown and learn from the things that could have tripped you up, the higher in the spirit you will become and the more power and authority the Lord can trust you with. You want to know why you have been through so much? You want to know why the Lord is still requiring so much from you? Maybe it is because He wants to release more power and authority to you but He is saying you have to come up higher to receive. *{And they heard a loud voice from heaven saying to them, "Come up here." And they ascended to heaven in a cloud, and their enemies saw them. Revelations 11:12 NKJV}*

Pastor Joanna is someone who knows what it feels like to have to keep stepping according to God's word even when at times she may want to give up or take a little break. I believe this book will give you that much need encouragement to keep on stepping. I believe those who live what they preach or write about are our best coaches. Who better to get in your face and say you must forgive that person who has hurt but someone who has had to forgive people who have hurt them.

What you are holding in your hand is a coach in a book form. Some of the words you read will get in your face and show you where you need to change your thoughts or actions and other times what you read will give you reinforcement, letting you know you are doing the right thing so keep it up! Regardless to however the Lord uses this book to speak to you know; the Lord has ordered your steps in this journey called life and NOW is the time for you to get to stepping! Place every negative experience under your feet by overcoming evil with good and prepare to be promoted thanks to your stepping-stones.

Ayanna L. Moore is a Wife, a Mother (Natural, Spiritual, Foster) ordained minister, mentor, transformation coach, author, publisher, businesswoman, and more, but the title she is most thankful for is Anointed Servant of the Most High God..
www.the-tstation.org

… STEPPING STONES : FAITH AT THE BREAKING POINT

DEDICATION

This book is dedicated to my Lord and Savior Jesus the Christ. You are the reason why I exist. I am so grateful for the opportunity you have given me and to write on your goodness and so this is just for you.

Even though this book is not just about women I would also like to dedicate this to all the women that are struggling through every pain and every delay. You haven't given up even though you are at the breaking point of your life and you recognize that you have the power to step over them.
Be Blessed!

STEPPING STONES : FAITH AT THE BREAKING POINT

ACKNOWLEDGMENTS

I thank the Lord for my husband Larry Birchett, Jr. Baby you have been such a great motivation in my life. Thank you for not holding me back. You always see the best in me, you are my blessing from the Lord!

To all my Children, I love you guys and I pray that the blessings of the Lord shower down on you all, for the rest of your lives. All of you keep me going.

INTRODUCTION

The Bible says to write the vision and make it plain. Here I was sitting in church one Sunday morning operating the camera while my hubby was bringing forth a powerful Word, when out of nowhere these words dropped in my spirit, *The Stepping Stones*.

I got paper and pen and began to write it down not knowing that it was to be the title for my next book.

I was amazed because when you can hear it and then see it you know that it is God.

Our Faith is activated and gets crazy according to what we believe. We will put all our trust in what we have faith and belief in.

After carefully seeking God and allowing Him to show me what He was trying to say to me I picked up the pace and began the journey.

The difference with this journey is that it is a Faith Walk; there is so much we can do when we walk by faith and not by sight.

Nobody said it would be easy, but through it all you will begin to recognize that it was all worth it.

I have come to recognize that there are many different people from all walks of life but personally for me I categorized them into three ways, The Faith Crawlers, The Faith Talkers and The Faith Walkers.

Follow me and learn where you fit into this walk.

THE STEPPING STONES

No matter who you are or where you are from, there will always be obstacles that try to hold you back. Well just to give a little clarity on what I mean by the title, stepping-stones is a pathway that takes you into your healing and wholeness.

There will come a time for all of us when we have some form of pain in our life both naturally and spiritually. Pain is sometimes good because without it you would not be able to recognize the stones that are there to strengthen our walk with Christ.

When you are serving God, believe it or not you will have a cross to bear. We have to find a way to look at these obstacles or crosses as stepping stones.

Helen Keller, the famous blind author and speaker, said: "Character cannot be developed in ease and quiet. Only through experience of trial and suffering can the soul be strengthened, vision cleared, ambition inspired and success achieved. Silver is purified in fire and so are we. It is in the most trying times that our real character is shaped and revealed."

As you take this journey to overcome the obstacles in life, remind yourself that these light afflictions are but only for a moment and the pain you bear now will bring a greater glory if we faint not.

If I was to begin to tell you my life's trials we would not be able to print this book it would be too many pages, and I know someone reading this can relate. But let me explain to you that even though I wrote the book "Defeat Was Never an Option" there are still trials that I am enduring and it is through all my pains and trials that I begin to see the hand of God move in my life.

Nobody said walking with the Lord would be easy, and I know you might say – But you are a Pastor. Well! Even leaders have needs, your position does not exempt anyone from being tried in the fire. Jesus was the ultimate example.

He is God in the flesh yet He was crucified on the cross just because of who He is.

It does not matter your age or gender , your destiny has already been decided by the Lord but there are some stones in the way that you have to step over.

Do you want to walk in your God given purpose? Well, I can tell you right now you will not make it if you are driven by your emotions and it won't be an easy task. So get ready to step over these stones in faith.

STEPPING STONES : FAITH AT THE BREAKING POINT

STEPPING INTO PURPOSE

Purpose is not picked up off the shelf or earned from reading a book. In all our lives we have to understand that there is a reason for us to be here.

There are some people who are still searching for their purpose but the truth be told is that when you are a child of God You should already know your purpose. Our purpose is to glorify the Lord by worshipping Him, loving Him and loving on His people. That is our God given purpose.

TD Jakes quoted on the Oprah Winfrey show "Many times we are pushed into functioning in an area that is not our highest and best use because someone needed us to be something we were not created to be." Don't base your life after what people are telling you that you are. God has a purpose for each of us and you will not find out what it is overnight.

The Spirit of God is always ready to do a new thing so always be prepared to move at the sound of God's commands. Be Spiritually ready and never depend on someone else's faith. I say this because walking with God is a personal thing when you elevate your faith purpose will be birthed.

We cannot quit just because the stones are piling up before us. After writing my first book "Defeat Was Never An Option" it gave me some hope because now I had to live the words that I spoke over my life. I cannot give up. If you are like me and you know that there is more in you, more to be used for the Kingdom, then I dare you take this first step with me. Step over fear and step into your purpose. Remember, God hath not given us a spirit of fear but of power, love and a sound mind. (2 Timothy 1:7)

In the summer of 2012 the Lord decided a different path for my family that caused a transition in the natural and also in the spiritual realm. My husband who is in the military was given orders and we had to relocate to Carlisle, Pennsylvania where it would be easier for him to commute. But in the midst of that He was also promoted and ordained as Pastor and due to the move the Lord spoke to his heart to begin the ministry, Harvest House Restoration Center. And so on July

8, 2012 the first service was conducted in the comfort of our own home.

Now, let me explain something to you, I was a cast out, I never knew that God had me in mind to be the First Lady to anyone. But one thing I know is that nothing catches Him by surprise. So I made up in my mind that it must be all for His glory. So this was the beginning of a purposeful journey.

When your mind is made up and you have decided that it's all about Jesus nothing else matters. You will not worry about the pit that the enemy is digging for you because if you should fall in, the same God that delivered Daniel is always right on time.

Say after me ~ Lord I am going all the way with you and these bumps and bruises will be the motivation that I will need to push me into my full purpose.

STEPPING STONES : FAITH AT THE BREAKING POINT

SILENCE IS GOLDEN

One of the most difficult seasons in the life of a Christian is when God seems silent. And to be honest, those seasons when God seems silent are usually when we think we need Him to speak the most.

I found myself going through a very difficult financial crisis at one point in my life. I prayed and fasted but there was no answer. I decided that no matter what things looked like I would have to trust God.

During the silence of relocating I found myself getting frustrated, weary as they say, but I thank God for His Holy Spirit because He began to minister to me even through the silence. I was at a place in my life that I was feeling lonely. Yes I had my husband but Joanna always liked to have everyone around. However, in the silence I heard the Spirit say when we are in Him, Standing alone is not possible. Why? Because He is always there. So do not mistake the quiet times for being alone just understand that it is time to receive.

God is usually silent to us when we are in a trial. Indeed, I have found that the silence of God and my inability to understand Him can, in itself, become a greater trial than any circumstance.

Here I was struggling with trying to figure out what is my purpose. One morning while I was in worship the Lord revealed to me that we all are waiting on God for something, but we have to be properly positioned (spiritually) so that when God releases the miracle, we are at the place to receive.

But in order to receive first we have to begin our day with praise, worship, and true submission to God. Why?
Because praise activates his ear to hear, then worship moves his heart and submission releases his perfect will for our lives.

So in the silence the Lord still speaks expressively and I started to realize that it really doesn't matter how long you are saved or what title or position you hold, what is important is your walk with God. In the midst of the silence doubt also began to creep in. All the questions were in my mind. Lord are you there? I preach week after week and I tell your people to trust you, but do I really trust you?

The silence taught me to trust God. Trusting Him with everything in me despite how the situation looked. Despite how I felt, I learned to look past myself and tap into the realm of the Spirit. And it was right there that He showed me that the same silence that I felt around me is how He desires my spirit to be. There is nothing like a woman that knows her value.

How a woman looks to God is more important than any other quality she possesses. The beauty that God sees in us will be important when we stand before Him. God values a quiet spirit in a woman. Ladies please know your role and allow the quiet times to bring you closer to God as He is strengthening your spirit.

It is the job of the enemy to disturb our peace and as we go through life day by day, just remember that you are God's masterpiece and even in His silence it brings revelation. So join me and step over the stone of doubt and step into His rest.

STEPPING STONES : FAITH AT THE BREAKING POINT

FAITH CRAWLERS

I remember when the Lord pressed on my heart to write my first book. It was a struggle. I say this because after all that I had been through I was at a place in my life where I was so ashamed to share with others what I had to endure. But I am so grateful to God that no matter where I am from or what I have done I have been redeemed by his blood.

Now when we talk about a faith crawler one might say that it could be referring to someone that just got saved but I beg to differ. A faith crawler is someone that is saved, sanctified and filled with the Holy Spirit. In other words they speak the word with no knowledge of it and will not display faith that works.

The Word of God states in Romans 12:3 *"For I say, through the grace given unto me, to every man that is among you, not to think of himself more highly than he ought to think; but to think soberly, according as God hath dealt to every man the measure of faith."* In order for you to walk by faith, you have to step out of "YOU".

Yes! looking beyond what you can see in the natural and focusing on the things that are Spiritual. Taking your emotions, your fears, and your doubts out of the way and relying wholly on the power of God in our life.

I am not saying that this will be easy but these challenges that we face are the things that make life somewhat more interesting, and no matter how big it gets we can step over them.

Sometimes our disadvantage is to our advantage, so we can show the world that there are no limits in God. In the book of Matthew 4:1 it declares And he said to them, *"Follow me, and I will make you fishers of men."* The reason why the fishes might not be catching your bait could be that it's not thrown in Faith.

Faith is one of the most powerful sources that God has given us, so if you are a faith crawler , you will not see the results that you are expecting because you are only living on the measure of faith that has been given to you. Actually you have to step it up higher. You have to put your faith in overdrive. A faith that leans on God Himself and not on your own understanding. We are sometimes challenged to believe that good answers are out there. It takes courage to press through the intellectual pain of questioning, seeking, learning, and stretching. I believe Jesus when He said He'll never leave us or forsake us. And that includes even when we question Him. Or as Paul said, even when we are faithless, God remains faithful.

Whatever is not of faith is sin, nothing will happen!

Join me and step over your doubts, insecurities and fears and allow the Power of God to consume you as you take this leap of faith!

STEPPING STONES : FAITH AT THE BREAKING POINT

FAITH TALKERS

We are living in a time when we have to get a personal relationship with the Lord. Knowing God through experience is radically different than knowing about Him from a theology textbook. This walk with God supersedes book knowledge and reaches to the core of our personal experiences with Him on a daily basis. If you have never had sickness in your body and experienced the healing hand of Jehovah Rophe, if you were never being evicted and Jehovah Jireh had to step in, then I dare say that you are a faith talker. Some people might not agree with me but I am a living testimony that GOD never fails.

No matter what your situation may look like today, your tomorrow is brighter when you have a personal relationship with the LORD. Faith is not just telling others you have it but allowing it to be visible in your life.

Everyone can say "I have faith" but the question is are you a talker or the just that live by faith?

I remember when God called my husband Larry Birchett Jr. to shepherd his own flock, and you would have thought that we would be in Philadelphia or New Jersey somewhere, but no! He said Carlisle! Now after all of my years being in this country I had never heard of Carlisle, but every mission that God has designed for us requires faith.

Now this is when our faith was being tested. I know for a fact that we had already said *Lord use us for your glory*. Were we just faith talkers? Because now the real task had began. Were we going to step over the obstacles in our way or were we going to give up without even trying?

Personally for me I have been through some rough and rocky roads on this walk with Christ but He was there all the time. To take everything and go to a strange place and begin what God wanted was a huge stone in our way but God! Yes I say huge stone because as much as we talked faith now we had to and have to live it and beloved it is not as easy as it sounds, but it is possible with the Lord on your side.

So we moved to Carlisle started services in our home and to be honest besides a few visitors here and there for the first couple months it was just me, my husband and the kids. But it was ok because the one thing I know is that God has connected me with a man of God that is full of faith. My husband would teach and preach the Word like it was hundreds of members there in our den.

So I say this to encourage someone, stop looking at where you are now, because you can rest assured that where you are now is temporal. His Word declares that your latter will be greater than your past. So do yourself a favor right where you are step over your past and open your mouth and declare that you are moving into your new season, you are no longer a talker but now you have stepped into the next dimension by faith.

STEPPING STONES : FAITH AT THE BREAKING POINT

FAITH WALKERS

We walk by faith, Not by sight ~ 2 Cor. 5:7

"Faith Walker" Yes Lord! After walking with the Lord for the past 14 years I have never felt so sure of anything in my life, I am at a place in my God where I am walking by Faith and not sight.

In order for anyone to step over something it has to be in your way and sometimes the enemy will make that thing look gigantic. But the last time I heard, even giants can be stepped over, *"the bigger they are the harder they fall."*

The obstacles of life are the stepping-stones and even though they seem like giants before us rest assured that God's Grace is sufficient.

I have been an unworthy benefactor of His love and favor but I am thankful for grace and even though it seems as though you have lost, I encourage somebody today to know that it is all working together for our good. All of it.

God desires our faith to be visible. He is a teacher and so He has left us the best book of faith, the Bible, which is our textbook to glory!

Understand this, fear fights against faith and it is fear's job to hold faith captive. We know this because it's through the wisdom and knowledge of the Holy Spirit that we walk this thing out. A man or woman of faith is not a crawler neither are they just talkers but their life is a living testament that faith is the substance of things hoped for and the evidence of things not seen. So therefore fear is a spirit and we have the remedy to defeat it.

I believe that each of us has a date with destiny so we have to learn how to step over the stones that are in our way. Break them if you may, but we have to cross over.

I was surfing the internet one day and saw this quote *"Faith is deliberate confidence in the character of God whose ways you may not understand at the time"* ~ *Oswald Chambers*

When you are a Faith Walker even your very thoughts bring

forth manifestation. I was sitting at home one day and was a bit troubled in my Spirit because sometimes the cares of life will try hard to bring you into captivity if you allow it. So I began to think on the scripture that my husband taught us in Bible Study. *Philippians 4:8 "Finally, brethren, whatsoever things are true, whatsoever things are honest, whatsoever things are just, whatsoever things are pure, whatsoever things are lovely, whatsoever things are of good report; if there be any virtue, and if there be any praise, think on these things."* About a few seconds later my phone rang and it was my husband, he was at work and was thinking about me. The words that he began to speak into my life was on time. I was so encouraged.

Many of us say that we are Christians, but our lives and our priorities indicate otherwise. Jesus put it this way "By their fruits you will know them." Do people pick grapes from thorn bushes or figs from thistles? Of course not, every good tree bears good fruit and rotten tree bears bad fruit. A good tree cannot bear bad fruit nor can a rotten tree bear good fruit. Every tree that does not bear good fruit will be cut down and thrown into the fire. So by their fruits you will know them. *Not everyone who says to me, 'Lord, Lord,' will enter the kingdom of heaven, but only the one who does the will of my Father in heaven. Many will say to me on that day, 'Lord, Lord, did we not prophesy in your name? Did we not drive out demons in your name? Did we not do mighty deeds in your name?' Then I will declare to them solemnly, I never knew you. Depart from me, you evildoers.*(Matthew 7:16–23).

As a faith walker you are a follower of Christ and because of that God expects those who claim to be followers of Jesus Christ to live differently from those who are not living in His will. We have to live what we preach. We are faith walkers and the point is that we often fail to realize just how much the world influences the way we think, act, speak and demonstrate love. The proof is that what we say we believe we don't do. We are children of the MOST high God so we have to think and act differently. We have to let our words bring forth manifestations and that is only possible when we begin to let go of being faith crawlers, faith talkers and becoming faith walkers. To walk by faith is to know that you're never truly taking a risk. Faith gives you the inner ability to see something greater than where you are right now because where you are now is not where you will be tomorrow. You can trust me on that.

God is getting ready to begin to break the high places. Faith walkers are you ready? Come on step!

FAITH TO TRUST

Now a man came up to Jesus and asked, "Teacher, what good thing must I do to get eternal life?"
"Why do you ask me about what is good?" Jesus replied. "There is only one who is good. If you want to enter life, obey the commandments."
"Which ones?" the man inquired.
Jesus replied, "Do not murder, do not commit adultery, do not steal, do not give false testimony, honor your father and mother, and love your neighbor as yourself."
"All these I have kept," the young man said. "What do I still lack?"
Jesus answered, "If you want to be perfect, go, sell your possessions and give to the poor, and you will have treasure in heaven. Then come, follow me."
When the young man heard this, he went away sad, because he had great wealth. ~ Matthew 19:16-22

There is so much that we can take from this scripture but I want to share with someone today that whatever you put your trust in shows your faith.

The young man in the story trusted in his riches and was not able to shift that trust to where it really should've been, in God.

What or who is your trust in?

I ask that question because I can remember waiting on God for years to bless me with my permanent residency and to be honest no money or no natural source or connection would be able to help me to receive it. But one thing for sure is that my faith was on trial.

Nothing is harder than knowing that what you are waiting on or going through is going to teach you to have Faith in God. Sometimes God will hold back the blessing just so that we will have no other choice but to Trust in Him, we have to really be souled out for the Lord be walking by faith (2 Corinthians 5:7)

Faith has to be tested and tried, in all honesty the real trial of faith is not that we find it difficult to trust in God but rather that God's character must be proven as trustworthy in our hearts.

My waiting caused me to feel like Job, though He slay me yet will I trust him ~ (Job 13:15). But through every test and every trial I could not lose hope. I had to remember that faith must be in the unseen before it can be applied to the things you can see. It is cultivated through personal communion with the Lord. Your relationship with Him is the most important aspect of your faith walk. You cannot see God but He will reveal Himself to you through His Word, by the power of the Holy Spirit.

If you are going through a challenging time in your life, join the club. They that are godly must suffer persecution, so turn your fear into faith and get ready to step over your unbelief. Begin to trust in the Lord. Unleash your Faith in God.

ced Stones : Faith at the Breaking Point

STEPPING STONES : FAITH AT THE BREAKING POINT

STEPPING FORWARD

But Lot's wife looked back, and she became a pillar of salt.~ Genesis 19:26

One morning while I was in worship the Lord revealed to me that we have to watch the people that are in our circle and recognize the takers, the makers and the builders.

You cannot allow everyone in your space. It will get crowded with the wrong crew. We have to open our spiritual eyes and see in the spirit that not because someone says they love you means that they are for real! I have to call it just like it is because for too long people have allowed the wrong people that I call "frienemies" to invade their spaces and they will fill the void that is meant for someone else. A void that only

God can fill.

People that are assigned to you they got your back because they are the builders. However, there are people that are not attached to you that will ride your tail because they are takers. These people will fill the space that is not meant for them because they are in it for what they can get. They will even ride your anointing. Watch as well as pray and don't allow everyone in your space. I have had so many people in and out of my life and please note I am talking about friends. And yes I would always call them friends. Well, after so many bad and hurtful experiences I have learned, (can somebody say learned) that whatever hurt I go through it is because I have allowed it and after all the past experiences that we have been through there has to be a point when enough is enough.

When you have a relationship with the Father, it brings peace of mind, joy to the fullest and love with no limits.

The story of Lot's wife is a familiar one and I used this because so many times God desires for us to move forward. But we are stuck in the same old thing, holding on to things and people that He is trying to take us from. We tend to be scared to let go, but that very thing or person that you are holding on to could sometimes be what is holding you back.

My beloved, God desires to take us higher but we have to be properly positioned (spiritually) so that when God releases the miracle, we are at the place to receive.

Let me take the liberty to say that you are asking God for more but He is waiting on you! He desires more of you. Not just our gifts but all of us. Forgetting those things behind and moving forward to receive what He has in store for you and I. Don't get worked up because you've failed in the past. As quoted by my husband, *Pastor Larry Birchett Jr.* ~ *"God will use your Failures as Fertilizers for your Future."*

You are destined for greatness so step away from the past and step forward into your future. Come on step!

GET BETTER NOT BITTER

"See to it that no one misses the grace of God and that no bitter root grows up to cause trouble and defile many." (Heb. 12:15)

Getting better not bitter is easily said than done, have you ever had someone hurt you so bad that you can feel the pain deep down and you know that you have to act differently? Maybe you have not but let me tell you this, it's one thing to get hurt but the true test is how we react even while we are being mistreated.

In all Jesus' anguish and pain He had the Authoritative Power to stop it, but instead He endured it to the end. There will be times in all our lives that we have to bear every hurt, every pain, every hatred, every pressure but know that your latter will be greater after the test.

Your tests are designed to catapult you into your purpose so no matter what beloved, you have to understand that when hard times come, we can always make the choice to feel sorry for ourselves and become bitter. We always have that choice. But as the young woman in the story reminds us, we always have another choice as well. We have the choice to see the light and joy in life rather than allowing ourselves to focus on the dark. We have the choice to learn from our trials, allowing them to refine our character and help us become a stronger and more loving person. I am not saying that when someone hurts us that it does not hurt but what I would like to get you to see is that you have to grin and bear it.

Getting better means that you are humbled by the Lord and no matter what stunts the enemy pulls you are not ignorant to his devices.

Even while I was in the process of finishing this book I was discouraged. Sometimes we allow our hearts to open too quickly and the Bible clearly tells us to "guard our hearts". But no matter what tricks the enemy comes with I am a child of the King. So I have to continue to love in spite of. You can do it too.

Come with me and let us step over bitterness so we can get

better. Bitterness has no place in our hearts. What are you waiting for? Step!

STEPPING OVER TEMPTATION

No temptation has overtaken you that is not common to man. God is faithful, and He will not let you be tempted beyond your ability, but with the temptation he will also provide the way of escape, that you may be able to endure it.~ 1 Cor. 10:13

Temptation is the urge to sin. We're judged by the degree to which we thwart our temptations. Because of humanity's sinful nature, everyone, at some point, fails to resist their temptations but I am here to help you because when we begin to go through different temptations whether in our mind or in the physical we begin to lose heart. But I believe that it's God's desire for us to be spiritually strengthened so that we don't faint and fall into the enemies traps. The Bible declares *"No temptation has overtaken you that is not common to man." (1 Corinthians 10:13).*

One thing that we need to know is that temptation is from the enemy but allowed by God, because He knows how much we can bear. When we see things happening in our lives we can rest assured that God is still in control. Too many times we see great men and women of God fall into sin. That's because we have to try our best to be who God has called us to be. I am not saying that we can stop temptations. No! But we can avoid falling into the traps. Here are a few strategies I would like to share from a Biblical point of view.

1. First you have to have a **Prayer** life. Prayer leads to praise and this activates God's ear to hear.
2. Then you have to **Use the Word** of God. Thy Word have I hid so I would not sin against thee.
3. Know your weaknesses **and run. This brings submission to the Lord and allow you to see you.**
4. And lastly, have good **accountability. You have to have true people that will cover you and make sure that you are in the will of the Father.**

There is a way that seems right to man but the end is destruction. No matter what we have to understand that we will always be tempted. But I hear the Lord saying, don't worry because we are secure when we are in Him. He always has a way of escape.

We must all realize that you probably will fall into temptation on occasion, but that is no reason for anyone to quit their walk with Christ. Don't accept your sin as if it doesn't matter, but also realize that you have a choice in your future actions.

Hey you, step past that temptation. Look at it as though it is a stone and step over!

SURRENDER YOU

We never know what God has in store for us and I say this because there are some places and positions that some of us will be placed in that does not require eloquence of speech, a major degree or any of the man made requirements. All God needs is your will to line up to His and that is called "I surrender."

To surrender means to cease resistance and submit to authority. How can we say we surrender when we are so caught up in us, my ministry, my money, my this, my that. The goal of every Christian should be to become Christ-like and to live life with the courage, compassion, power and principles of Jesus. The greatest example was when Jesus surrendered Himself completely to the will of the Father by offering His life as a sacrifice for you and I. Now with that being said have you totally surrendered your will to the Father? This is really between you and Him.

Sometimes we shut down because we find ourselves in the court of the "public opinion" and we underestimate the power of God in our lives. But if we really want to learn how to step over the pains, obstacles and giants that are in our path we have to shut everything out and surrender our will to His. The power on the inside of us will allow our purpose to be birthed.

We make all these plans summer vacations, college degree, children college fund, but the truth be told, God is the one that decides our destiny. So why not yield to His will.

When we yield to the will of the Lord our pain propels us to walk into purpose and then your passion gets aroused so therefore the power of God is now more evident in your life and you will go forth with His authority.

Sometimes God allows you to go through trying situations that he doesn't allow to change because He wants you to change your outlook, not your situation.

When the enemy recognizes that you are a threat to the Kingdom, you best believe that he gets busy, and as children of God we cannot get passive or emotional we have to stand our ground. Even during your process of surrendering, there will be struggles, but through every struggle you will begin to see God change you in the midst of the struggles.

Who said that it would be easy? Well my beloved this walk with God has taught me how to be passive, be still and wait on Him. Can God trust you to praise Him while He has you in wait mode? Will you surrender your will to His?

CHARACTER IS KEY

Therefore, since we have been justified by faith, we have peace with God through our Lord Jesus Christ. Through him we have also obtained access by faith into this grace in which we stand, and we rejoice in hope of the glory of God. More than that, we rejoice in our sufferings, knowing that suffering produces endurance, and endurance produces character, and character produces hope, and hope does not put us to shame, because God's love has been poured into our hearts through the Holy Spirit who has been given to us. ~ Romans 5:1-5

Abraham Lincoln said, "Reputation is the shadow. Character is the tree." Our character is much more than just what we try to display for others to see. It is who we are even when no one is watching. Good character is doing the right thing because it is right to do what is right.

One might wonder what is the importance of good character. I am here to tell you that when you are a man or woman of good character your fruit speaks for itself, your word is bond as they say and you will be a ready vessel for the Lord to use.

You will be walking by faith and not sight because faith justifies us. We are being tested on every side because God has purpose in store for us. He is using different obstacles to build good character in us.

One thing that I have learned in this life is that no matter how much money you have in the bank or what position you hold, it means nothing if all people see is your bad character.

So they stepped on your toes and did not show any compassion, are you going to be mad at the world all day?

A good character is better than having all the money in the bank. The word of God makes it plain that *"For we are His workmanship, created in Christ Jesus for good works, which God prepared beforehand that we should walk in them" (Ephesians:2:10)*

As long as we are human, our character is not firm and it is not permanent. We can change our minds and behavior. We can make mistakes and learn from them. We can learn from the fruits of our right and wrong choices because our past experiences teaches us wisdom and brings us into maturity to build our character.

Since we can change our minds and repent of our errors, God can change us even more and create in us the will and the capacity to steadfastly choose what is right over what is wrong. *For it is God who works in you both to will and to do for His good pleasure"* (Philippians 2:13).

Whether you are saved or not it is always a good thing to have good character. Now when you come to Christ no matter what you have done it is in the sea of forget me and leave me alone, oh yes! There is now no condemnation to them that are in Christ Jesus. Why? Because we no longer walk after the flesh but rather the Spirit. In the midst of finding you there will be people that will tell you that you are not worthy. But look them in the eye (in love) and let them know that you were bought with a price. You are a son and daughter of the King of all kings and you are fearfully and wonderfully created in God's image.

Walk as Jesus walked, talk as He did and your fruit will speak for itself.

VICTORY

But thanks be to God, which giveth us the victory through our Lord Jesus Christ. ~ 1 Cor. 15:57

Victory, I like the sound of that. In life every story has an ending but in Christ every ending is a new beginning. So as we go through this life we should be very mindful of the fact that we are safe in His arms and no matter what stones are in our way, with Christ, we will step over them. We are justified by faith and even at the breaking point, we are still victorious.

I don't know about you but I had some giants to face and still facing but I believe the Bible tells us that "we are more than a conqueror". To be "more than a conqueror" means we not only achieve victory, but we are *overwhelmingly* victorious. Even if we get knocked down we know that we bounce right back. As the songwriter says *"we are a hard nut to crack."*

I want to encourage some and speak to others to let you know that no matter what , you are already a winner and you have the victory.

Don't wait for tomorrow to shout. Open up your mouth and spring forth His praises. Let the Praise begin.

This season is filled with much blessings and I can feel it in my spirit that something unusual is about to happen. And I am ready to receive. Know who you are. Live like it, walk like it and understand the principles of the Kingdom and you will begin to see the manifestation of His blessings.

No matter where you are reading this, shout NOW! Send up your praises! Praise Him because you have made it, the victory is already won.

JOANNA BIRCHETT

Now that you have stepped over the thorns that were hindering you, I challenge you that this next 21 days will bring forth Fruit because it is your due season.

Job 22:28 Thou shalt also decree a thing, and it shall be established unto thee: and the light shall shine upon thy ways.

We have often heard and read this passage of scripture but have you meditated on the meaning of this powerful word. Take this journey with me as we follow the lead of the Spirit and step into the next move of God for your life.

21 Days of Devotional

& Declarations

STEPPING STONES : FAITH AT THE BREAKING POINT

DAY 1

FAITH WALK

Now faith is the substance of things hoped for, the evidence of things not seen. ~ Hebrews 12:1

Have you ever woke up and stop to think, Will this work out? Or how can I get to this point?
Well, I have. And every time this happens God has a way of allowing me to see that He got this! We go through this phase unexpectedly, not realizing that we are doubting the power of God in our lives.

We, according to the Apostle Paul in 2 Corinthians chapter 5, "Walk by faith and not by sight." Paul writing to the Galatians in chapter 2 says, "We live by the faith of the Son of God." Hebrews 11 says, "Without faith it is impossible to please God, and faith is the substance of things hoped for, the evidence of things not seen." So we believe and we live by faith. Faith is the dominating feature of the life of every Christian because we have to put our trust entirely in what we cannot see.

What do I mean by that? We trust in a God we have not seen. We embrace a death and resurrection we have not seen. We trust in a justification we have not seen. And we look for a fulfillment in eternal heaven, which we have not seen. And so we live by faith. It is not blind faith, it is faith based on evidence. And the evidence for our faith that anchors our faith is the Scripture, the Word of God, because this tells us all we need to know and it is a true Word. It is a sure Word. It is an unassailable Word. But nonetheless, we live by faith.

DECLARATION

I decree and declare that I am a Faith walker. I walk by Faith and not by sight and I shall live to declare the goodness of the Lord in the land of the living in Jesus Name. Amen

Sign Your Name_____

DAY 2

COMMIT IT ALL TO HIM

For which cause I also suffer these things; nevertheless I am not ashamed. For I know whom I have believed, and am persuaded that he is able to keep that which I have committed unto him against that day. ~ 2 Timothy 1:12

This is a new day. New mercies are streaming in your home, on your job, everywhere you go and no matter what the situation might look like I urge you today before you do anything else, to stop right where you are and commit your day to the lord. Yes!
He will keep that which you commit unto him and whether it's sickness, your marriage, your walk, your finances, your family, your ministry, we can go on and on, no matter what it is he shall keep it.

The reasons we are not seeing the power of God evident in our situations is because of us. We have to wake up every morning and commit our day unto the Lord and the God of Abraham, Isaac and Jacob will keep that which concerns thee. I charge you today to stop whatever you are doing and open your heart and say after me:

DECLARATION

Lord, I commit this day unto you. My life, my family, my all walk with me today. Lord and allow your promises to birth forth in me to be used for Your glory. I am your son/daughter **SAY YOUR NAME**
And I am sorry for neglecting your Word. So I begin today to commit my days unto you and I know you will keep it all. In Jesus name. Amen!

Sign Your Name_____

DAY 3

BUSY DOING NOTHING

³⁸ now it came to pass, as they went, that he entered into a certain village: and a certain woman named Martha received him into her house.

³⁹ and she had a sister called Mary, which also sat at Jesus' feet, and heard his word.

⁴⁰ but Martha was cumbered about much serving, and came to him, and said, Lord, dost thou not care that my sister hath left me to serve alone? Bid her therefore that she help me.

⁴¹ and Jesus answered and said unto her, Martha, Martha, thou art careful and troubled about many things:

⁴² but one thing is needful: and Mary hath chosen that good part, which shall not be taken away from her. ~ Luke 10:38-42 (KJV)

Mary and Martha were two sisters and when Jesus came to their home Martha was busy with the cares of life. She was distracted from what should have been her highest priority, that is learning from Jesus. But Mary stayed at Jesus' feet. The choice that Mary made was an eternally commendable choice that will never be taken away from her. Let me encourage someone today that being in God's presence brings a peace that surpasses all understanding. It does not matter what everyone else is doing, what matters is your relationship with God. Don't be in His presence and miss Him. Get busy for Jesus! That is the mandate on our lives. Today, we have to stay at His feet.

DECLARATION

Today I decree and declare the will of God for my life. I declare that I am the righteousness of God and in the name of Jesus I will become a warrior and not a worrier. Thank you Lord for instilling a Mary spirit in me. I surrender me to you today.

Sign Your Name_____

DAY 4

Warfare or Discipline

For whom the Lord loveth he chasteneth, and scourgeth every son whom he receiveth. ~Hebrews 12:6

So many times we jump to the conclusion that every time we find ourselves in a rough place that it is warfare. I agree that everything is spiritual, but when you are a child of God there are always consequences to your actions and there is no sin that goes unpunished. God loves us unconditionally and He will chastise us so we can get it together. He desires the best for you and I and no matter what we do it will never change His love for us. So I urge you today not to look at what you are going through, whether it's warfare or discipline, but rather learn from every lesson and mature your Spirit so that He is able to get the Glory from your life.

DECLARATION

I decree and declare that as of today I will allow the Lord to chastise me as He will and I will walk circumspectly in His commands as He leads and direct my path. In Jesus name, Amen.

Sign Your Name_____

DAY 5

PRAY YOUR WAY OUT

If my people, who are called by my name, will humble themselves and pray and seek my face and turn from their wicked ways, then I will hear from heaven, and I will forgive their sin and will heal their land. ~ 2 Chronicles 7:14

There is a call for prayer! Saints of God if you have never turned down your plates now is the time to get busy for Jesus by interceding for the nations. Sometimes we have to forget about ourselves and look to the hills from whence cometh our help. Clearly all your help is going to come from God! So I encourage you today to stop being busy doing nothing and if you don't have a relationship with the Lord and Savior

Jesus the Christ Begin today! The Word of God declares in Acts 7:56 "And said, Behold, I see the heavens opened, and the Son of man standing at the right hand of God." We are living in the end times and we have to get it right, tomorrow is not promised to none of us, so let us **stop** all the foolishness and get on our knees, there is **power** in **prayer**.

DECLARATION

My declaration today is that I am in a season that I know that I am on an assignment from the Lord. He has purpose for my Life. I am in His master plan and will not allow people's faces, funny faces or mean faces to stop my assignment.. I decree that everything that was stolen will be returned today in Jesus Name Amen.

Sign Your Name_____

DAY 6

WHAT IS MY PURPOSE

For I know the plans I have for you, declares the Lord, plans for welfare and not for evil, to give you a future and a hope. ~ Jeremiah 29:11

Purpose is not picked up off the shelf or earned from reading a book. In all our lives we have to understand that there is a reason for us being here.

When God created us He had greatness in mind and so because of that we have to go through the shaking, the pressing and the pain to find our true purpose.

As Bishop TD Jakes quoted "Many times we are pushed into functioning in an area that is not our highest and best use because someone needed us to be something we were not created to be." Don't base your life after what people are telling you that you are. The Spirit of God is always ready to do a new thing, so always be prepared to move at a moment's notice. Always be spiritually ready because we make all these plans but it's God who decides our destiny.

I believe that if we only humble ourselves and allow the Lord to build character in us that we would see that sometimes the things that we are stressed and worried about is nothing of importance. But as we submit our will to the Lord we will begin to walk as men and women of purpose.

Understand this my beloved, when God tests us it is to bring forth the purpose that He has instilled within us from the beginning, but on the other hand the enemy will tempt us so he can abort the plans of God for us. So we cannot allow him to play patter cake in our minds, instead allow the Holy Spirit to lead you and you will begin to see God's purpose bursting through.

The first thing we do when God speaks to us is critical. In John 21 Jesus told Peter what type of ministry he would have and the type of death he would suffer. Jesus began to pull back the curtain to his future, but instead of responding to what Jesus told him Peter began to look around at everyone else around him. Isn't that like some of us? God speaks expressively and we try to compare our assignment with others.

There is a place in God that we all must get to so purpose can be fulfilled but we will not get there if our focus is on the wrong things.

DECLARATION

I decree and declare today that I will fulfill the purpose that God has planned for my life. Have your way Lord, I am moving by your Spirit so Lord thank you for refocusing my focus. In Jesus Name.

Sign Your Name_____

DAY 7

DISCIPLINE 101

Now when the tempter came to Him, he said, "If You are the Son of God, command that these stones become bread." But He answered and said, "It is written, Man shall not live by bread alone, but by every word that proceeds from the mouth of God." ~ Matthew 4:3-4

As a young girl growing up my mother was a very disciplined person. She was not saved but she would make sure that she trained us up in the way we should grow. Many times in life even now as an adult I can remember the words of "Go to bed at 9", "make sure all the dishes are washed", and "get up and get ready for Church." These words never leave me. I could not wait to grow up to move out not knowing that one day I would have children of my own. So now that I am an adult I am learning that true discipline begins in you and that my mommy was on point.

Jesus was the ultimate example. When we look at how He was tempted by the devil but through it all He did not fall to His flesh. He set the pace to teach us that our spirits need discipline.

When there is spiritual discipline we will not be subject to the enemies devices.

DECLARATION

I decree and declare by the power of the Holy Spirit that I will discipline my self to do the will of the Father. Help me Lord to walk according to Your Word so that people can see Your light in me.

Sign Your Name_____

DAY 8

FROM BREAKOUT TO BREAKTHROUGH

Count it all joy, my brothers, when you meet trials of various kinds, for you know that the testing of your faith produces steadfastness. ~ (James 1:2–3)

So you are at the end of your last straw and you say *I quit. I give up. I just cannot do this anymore.* But I hear the Lord saying to you today, keep pressing, keep pursuing, because it's in your stretching that your faith is increased within you.

My brother and sisters faith that is not tested is not faith at all. This breaking will only place you into a place of rest in God.

Faith is like muscle tissue, if you stress it to the limit, it gets stronger, not weaker. That's what James means here. When your faith is threatened and tested and stretched to the breaking point, the result is a greater capacity to endure.

I am not saying that it will not be hard but with God ALL things are possible if we only believe. Break out of the box and allow the Lord to take you into your breakthrough.

DECLARATION

I am the righteousness of God and I decree and declare that this is my season to **break out** into my **breakthrough**. I speak this into the atmosphere and it is so in Jesus name. Amen!

Sign Your Name_____

Day 9

Faith That Moves

Behold, I am the Lord, the God of all flesh: is there any thing too hard for me? ~ Jeremiah 32:27

My beloved, you have made it to day 9, how have you been doing with the declaration challenge?

You are on the road to a faith recovery and you cannot turn back now. Remember this, faith raises your expectations and will not allow you to settle for less. So when God speaks to you, what you do next proves who whether you trust or believe. Do you have faith that obeys and move?

When we begin to exercise our faith we will see the next move of God in our lives. I am 100% sure of the fact that faith in God brings positive results. Jeremiah reminds us that there is nothing, absolutely nothing too hard for God. So with that being said, let us walk this thing out and concentrate on the Greater in us.

DECLARATION

In this atmosphere I declare that Faith is my portion. I have the ability to speak a thing and it shall be so in Jesus Name. Amen!

Sign Your Name_____

DAY 10

DO YOU KNOW YOUR WORTH

I will praise thee; for I am fearfully and wonderfully made: marvellous are thy works; and that my soul knoweth right well. ~ Psalm 139:14

Do you know who you are? Well as for me I am confident in one thing that I am SAVED, SANCTIFIED and HOLY GHOST FILLED and because of that I am a Force to be reckoned with. You might say Joanna you are too much, but yes! I am so much in God that I am confident of who I am. So please stop and begin to recognize who you are. I am a woman of worth, full of value, fearfully and wonderfully made. So therefore when you know your worth all the qualities of God will shine through you. There is no room for hate, envy , a get even spirit and/ or compromise, because the light of the Lord illuminates through your beautiful heart.

Anger, bitterness and the likes are not your portion.

Just like Jesus, you will have haters but love them regardless and no matter what, you have to allow the love of God to permeate in you so that it will be manifested around you. You are a man or woman of worth and it does not mean that you have a lot of money. Oh no! Your worth is your value. You are valuable to God. We are his signature masterpiece and because of that we have to recognize and understand that we are.

Have a Faith Filled day.

DECLARATION

I decree and declare that I am a man/woman of worth and by the power of the Holy Spirit I am going to be all that the Lord has spoken of me. I am no longer bound. I am free to declare the goodness of the Lord in the land of the living. In Jesus name!

Sign Your Name_____

DAY 11

STOP WORRYING

Be careful for nothing; but in every thing by prayer and supplication with thanksgiving let your requests be made known unto God. ~ Philippians 4:6-7

Mary and Martha were two sisters but Martha was troubled in her Spirit, she wanted things quickly, she was worried about everything, on the other hand Mary Had Peace of mind, even though things were not all good she stayed at the Masters feet, I want to encourage someone today, take it easy, God is in full control and He does not need your help. You are designed to win so do not allow the cares of life to tear you apart. Take a deep breath, relax and enjoy the ride. God is in charge and you best believe He is running the whole show anyway.

Our worries don't take God by surprise. He allows things to happen for two reasons:

1. For His Glory
2. For our Good

The word tells us that all things work together for good because we love the Lord and are called according to His purpose. Get over it, you cannot fix it, just trust and believe in God and when you trust you let go of everything.

DECLARATION

Say after me:

I decree and declare that worry is not in my vocabulary. I am walking in the power of His peace and no sickness, no finances, no weapon that is formed against me will prosper nor cause me to worry. I am who God says that I am in Jesus name. Amen!

Sign Your Name_____

DAY 12

CLOTHED IN FAVOR

His anger lasts only a moment. His favor lasts a lifetime. Weeping may last for the night, but there is a song of joy in the morning. ~ Psalm 30:5

Did you wake up this morning? Are you clothed in your right mind? Well! If your answer is yes to any of these questions that means you are clothed in **favor**.

Favor is for a lifetime and everyday that you are alive you have God's favor. Without faith, I can't please God. If I don't please God I cannot receive His favor. Not believing that God will do what He says, displeases Him. The reward in believing God brings His blessings and favor on our life.

So stop getting worried about the struggles that you can see because the great I Am is working behind the scene and His favor is more than enough for you. When you have God's

Favor you don't need money.

As you begin to bask in the presence of God understand that all we need is faith and favor.

DECLARATION

I come in agreement with you today that favor is your portion. You shall walk in favor, live in favor and wherever you go favor will follow you. Everything that I desire will be added unto me in Jesus Name.

Sign Your Name_____

DAY 13

NO SHORTCUTS

"We know that in all things God works for good with those who love him, those whom he has called according to his purpose." ~ Romans 8:28

You cannot live out someone else's testimony, there are no shortcuts with God. The word of God tells us to wait on the Lord and be of good courage, it never said to do whatever we will.

We all have great desires. I would love to be in that white BMW X6 with tan interior and never have to work another day and live comfortable. But I have learned that as long as I wait on the Lord He will grant me every desire of my heart as long as it is in His will. I know that the promises of God are yes and amen. There is nothing impossible with God so I will patiently wait on the Lord for every blessing that He has promised.

We cannot get anywhere if we envy other people or have jealousy in our hearts. When this is present then you best believe that you will not go further. One of the main problems in most ministries these days is that there is no submission. It is a word that people think is only meant for marriages. Growing up my mom always say "Short path draws blood, long path brings sweat". Over the years I had to learn that the hard way. There are no shortcuts to success, no not one. If Jesus bore the cross we have to bear ours.

DECLARATION

At the sound of my voice with the power of the Holy Spirit within me, I declare that you shall be all that God has spoken regarding you in His timing. And you will take the directions given unto you, in Jesus Name!

Sign Your Name_____

DAY 14

JUDGE NOT!

¹ Judge not, that ye be not judged.
² For with what judgment ye judge, ye shall be judged: and with what measure ye mete, it shall be measured to you again. Matthew 7:1-2

Your job isn't to judge. Your job isn't to figure out if someone deserves something or to decide who is right or wrong. Your job is to lift the fallen, restore the broken, and heal the hurting. We are such judgmental people and finding faults with others will get us nowhere. I assure you that if you begin to speak less negatively about others that you will begin to see that the faults that we find are destructive to us and not constructive at all.

Whenever you see a fault in a brother or a sister and you want to make them feel bad take a minute and think what would Jesus do in this situation?

DECLARATION

According to the book of Matthew 7:1 I have been ordered to judge not or I will be judged, so today I commit my life to speaking love no matter what. Thank you Lord for cleansing my heart in Jesus Name!

Sign Your Name_____

DAY 15

DIAMOND IN THE ROUGH

7 But we have this treasure in earthen vessels, that the excellency of the power may be of God, and not of us.
8 We are troubled on every side, yet not distressed; we are perplexed, but not in despair;
9 Persecuted, but not forsaken; cast down, but not destroyed;
10 Always bearing about in the body the dying of the Lord Jesus, that the life also of Jesus might be made manifest in our body. ~
2 Corinthians 4 7-10

The cutting of diamond requires specialized knowledge, tools, equipment, and techniques because of its extreme difficulty. These stones has to be strategically worked on to become a diamond and in the physical realm and in the spiritual realm only God has the capability to transform us from the natural into the supernatural.

No matter what you are going through always remember that you are being pruned for purpose. You are a diamond in the rough and because of that you have to endure the process.

During the process these steps are taken; *planning, cleaving, sawing, bruiting, polishing,* and *final inspection.*

Every step takes you higher so don't quit now. I don't have all the answers but I have been sent to tell you that your, pain process and pressure is for such a time as this. Hold on just a little while longer and you will run this race and finish strong. Yes you will.

Diamonds shine so begin to let your light shine for the Kingdom.

DECLARATION

I release growth into your life. May the fire of
God begin to burn in your heart burn away every rough area and I release the diamond in you in Jesus name.

Sign Your Name_____

DAY 16

MORE OF YOU- LESS OF ME

He must increase, but I must decrease.~ John 3:30

The more that we walk with the Lord, our relationship with Him gets deeper, closer, and sweeter.

There is nothing on this earth that entices me more than knowing that my soul is anchored in Christ. Where would we be without Him? What would we do if He did not show us His grace? These are questions that we should be asking ourselves and because of that I ask him to kill my flesh daily. Yes! Sometimes we get ahead of ourselves, we tend to forget that He is the source of our everything.

No one has arrived so none of us are exempt from asking the Lord to decrease us so that He can increase in our lives.

My husband says this all the time "Humility comes before Honor" and that is the key to becoming all that God has called you to be.

Die to self and live in the Spirit.

DECLARATION

I declare and decree that I the Spirit of the Lord live in me and I am blessed and highly favored by the King. I speak life over my life and as I decrease, goodness and mercy shall follow me and I shall see His power increase in and around me In Jesus name, Amen.

Sign Your Name_____

DAY 17

ARE YOU BOUND OR FREE

For sin shall not have dominion over you: for ye are not under the law, but under grace. ~ Romans 6:14

You are bound because you choose to be, so stop blaming other people for your lack of commitment and consistency. It's time to free yourself. You are bound because of you. Time to grow up!
Proverbs 16:3 "Roll your works upon the Lord [commit and trust them wholly to Him; He will cause your thoughts to become agreeable to His will, and] so shall your plans be established and succeed."

Sometimes your being bound is being caused by you because you are carrying the wrong people in your circle. It is time for a cleaning. Clean away the things and the people that hinder you. Step out in faith today and believe God for your freedom.

DECLARATION

Open your mouth and declare after me: I am free, no longer bound. There are no chains holding me. I am a child of the King and because of that I am A man/woman that is fitted for the Kingdom.
Can you feel the freedom?

Sign Your Name_____

DAY 18

ATMOSPHERE SHIFTER

and the priests could not perform their service because of the cloud, for the glory of the Lord filled the temple of God. ~ 2 Chronicles 5:14

TO Shift: To move or to cause (something or someone) to move to a different place, position, etc.

Another Definition: To change or to cause (something) to change to a different opinion, belief, etc.

In order for a shift to happen there must be an atmosphere of unified expectancy. Every time believers come together something is supposed to happen, meaning God has given us the power and authority to speak to sickness, lack, hurt, depression and they have to flee. These prayers prayer calls are not allowed by accident, everything has a purpose in God. So therefore if we enter a room filled with depressed folks we should not be affected because of who we are. We are atmosphere breakers! In other words we are anointed to bring change.

Open your heart today and begin to let the power of God come through you so that you can be a vessel that He uses to shift the Atmosphere.

DECLARATION

I affirm that every step I take will be ordered by the Lord. I order every door that is not of God to close and release every God ordained door to open in Jesus Name.

Sign Your Name_____

DAY 19

BE YOURSELF

For I say, through the grace given unto me, to every man that is among you, not to think of himself more highly than he ought to think; but to think soberly, according as God hath dealt to every man the measure of faith. ~ Romans 12:3

God works in different people in different ways. Some people grow rapidly, while others grow slowly. When we begin to compare ourselves with others we miss the move of God in our own lives.

Our focus should not be on comparing ourselves with others, but comparing ourselves with God's Word. Be who God has called you to be and the rest is history.

There is an uniqueness in all of us and we cannot change who we are but we can control who we become.

Stop complaining about what others have achieved and be

yourself!

DECLARATION

I am not Jealous of anyone. I will be all that the Lord has said I will be. I decree and declare that I am fearfully and wonderfully made in His Image. So by the power that lives in me I declare that I am the best me that I will ever be in Jesus Name, Amen!

Sign Your Name_____

DAY 20

WIN OR LOSE

But thanks be to God, who gives us the Victory through our Lord Jesus Christ. ~ 1 Corinthians 15:57

No one wants to lose, we all want to win but there is a time for everything under the sun. Sometimes in life you win and sometimes you lose, but with God you are already a winner. Isn't it amazing that we have the power to choose whether we win or lose? How many times are we placed in a position where it seems as though our backs are against the wall or that we are at a breaking point in life. I am here to tell you that Jesus did not seem to be a winner in His time and He even appeared to be a loser. If we would look at His physical existence we would think that He was just a man who was rejected, despised, and then murdered without a cause.

Isaiah 53:3-6, "He is despised and rejected of men; a man of sorrows, and acquainted with grief: and we hid as it were our faces from Him; He was despised, and we esteemed him not. Surely he hath borne our grief's, and carried our sorrows: yet we did esteem Him stricken, smitten of God, and afflicted. But he was wounded for our transgressions, He was bruised for our iniquities: the chastisement of our peace was upon Him; and with His stripes we are healed."

Never judge a book by it's cover. No matter what your situation may look like, know this, you are a winner in Christ Jesus!

DECLARATION

I decree and declare that according to Matthew 19:30 - But many who are first will be last, and many who are last will be first. I am a winner in Christ Jesus and no weapon that is formed against me shall prosper In Jesus Name, Amen!

Sign Your Name_____

DAY 21

IT IS FINISHED

I have fought a good fight, I have finished my course, I have kept the faith: ~ 2 Timothy 4:7

Just like Jesus when He was on the cross and He cried out "IT IS FINISHED" that is how you are supposed to feel right now. Every trial, every delay, every hurt is not meant to take you out. But you have to remember, that no matter what you have to go through, you already have the victory! Come on that is enough to give a praise and shout! You are destined to win and that is a fact. Like I told you before "defeat is and never should be an option". We have to take this by force. The word of God tells us in Matthew 11:12 "From the Days of John the Baptist until now, The Kingdom of Heaven suffered violence and the violent take it by force." What have the devil stolen from you? Come on open your mouth and declare in this atmosphere that devil no matter what you try, I am not intimidated or troubled by your foolish devices. I have come to tell you today that every struggle, every hurt , every unforgiveness, every pressure, every pain, can no longer reside here. It is finished!

I now step over my obstacles and step into my new season in Jesus name and it is so Amen!

DECLARATION

I decree and declare that **it is finished**.

Whatever it is it's done in Jesus name. Amen!

Sign Your Name_____

ABOUT THE AUTHOR

Pastor Joanna Birchett is the Co-Pastor to her wonderful Husband Pastor Larry Birchett, Jr. at the Harvest House Restoration Center, located in Carlisle PA.

She is the CEO of Gospel 4 U Network and a Mighty vessel that is ready and always willing to be used by the Lord whether through the art of Dance or allowing the Lord to speak through her.

For inquiries or Speaking engagements please contact her at info@gospel4unetwork.com and visit her website at www.gospel4unetwork.com

STEPPING STONES : FAITH AT THE BREAKING POINT

www.ingramcontent.com/pod-product-compliance
Lightning Source LLC
Chambersburg PA
CBHW071143090426
42736CB00012B/2201